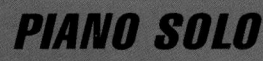

MARVEL

AVENGERS
AGE OF ULTRON

**MUSIC FROM THE
MOTION PICTURE SOUNDTRACK**

Images and artwork © 2015 MARVEL
MARVEL SUPERHEROES MUSIC

ISBN 978-1-4950-2953-0

DISTRIBUTED BY

HAL•LEONARD®
CORPORATION

7777 W. BLUEMOUND RD. P.O. BOX 13819 MILWAUKEE, WI 53213

In Australia Contact:
Hal Leonard Australia Pty. Ltd.
4 Lentara Court
Cheltenham, Victoria, 3192 Australia
Email: ausadmin@halleonard.com.au

For all works contained herein:
Unauthorized copying, arranging, adapting, recording, Internet posting, public performance,
or other distribution of the printed music in this publication is an infringement of copyright.
Infringers are liable under the law.

Visit Hal Leonard Online at
www.halleonard.com

*Not featured in film.

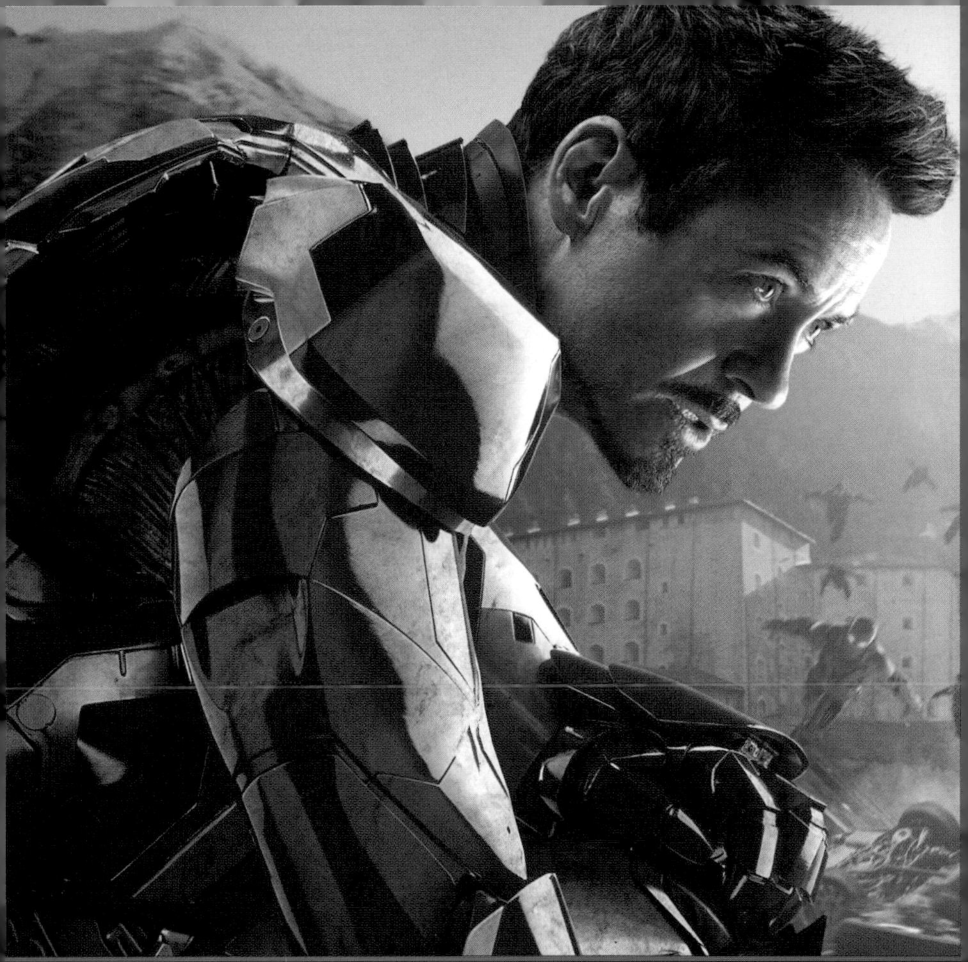

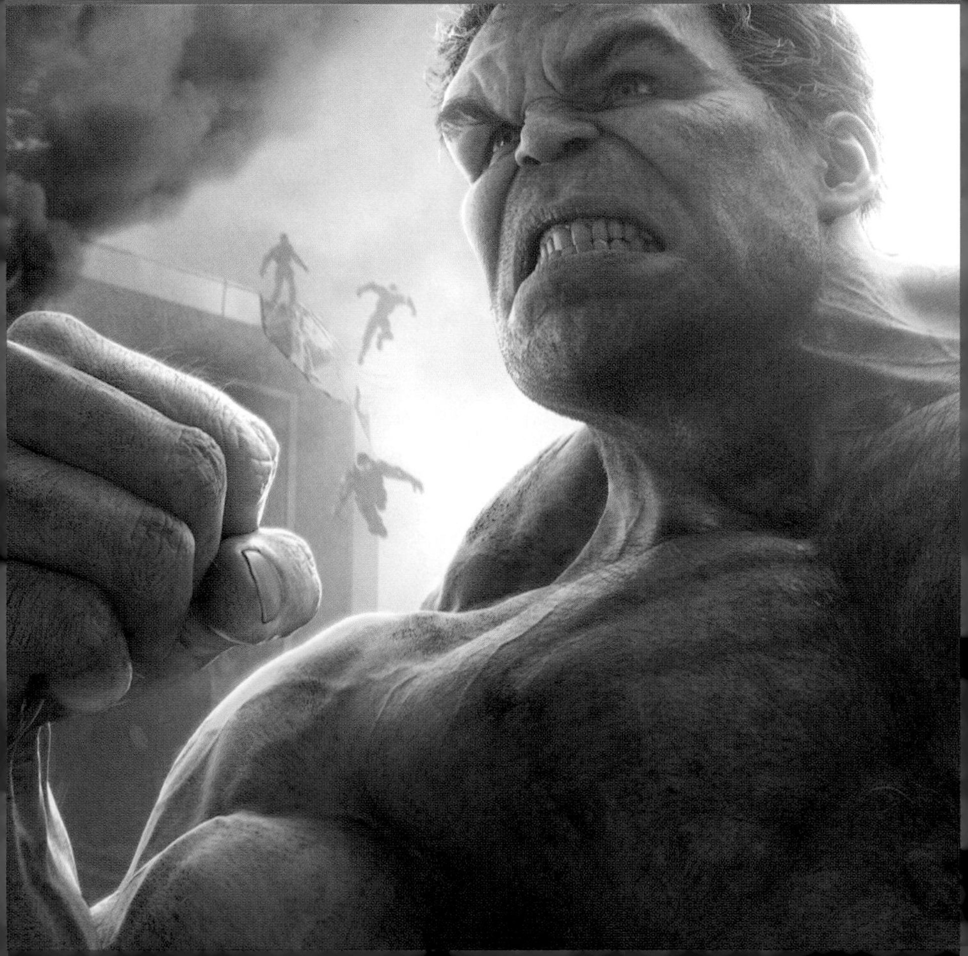

HEROES

Music by
DANNY ELFMAN

© 2015 MARVEL Superheroes Music
All Rights Reserved   Used by Permission

RISE TOGETHER

Music by
BRIAN TYLER

Moderately, in 2

© 2015 MARVEL Superheroes Music
All Rights Reserved   Used by Permission

FARMHOUSE

Music by
DANNY ELFMAN

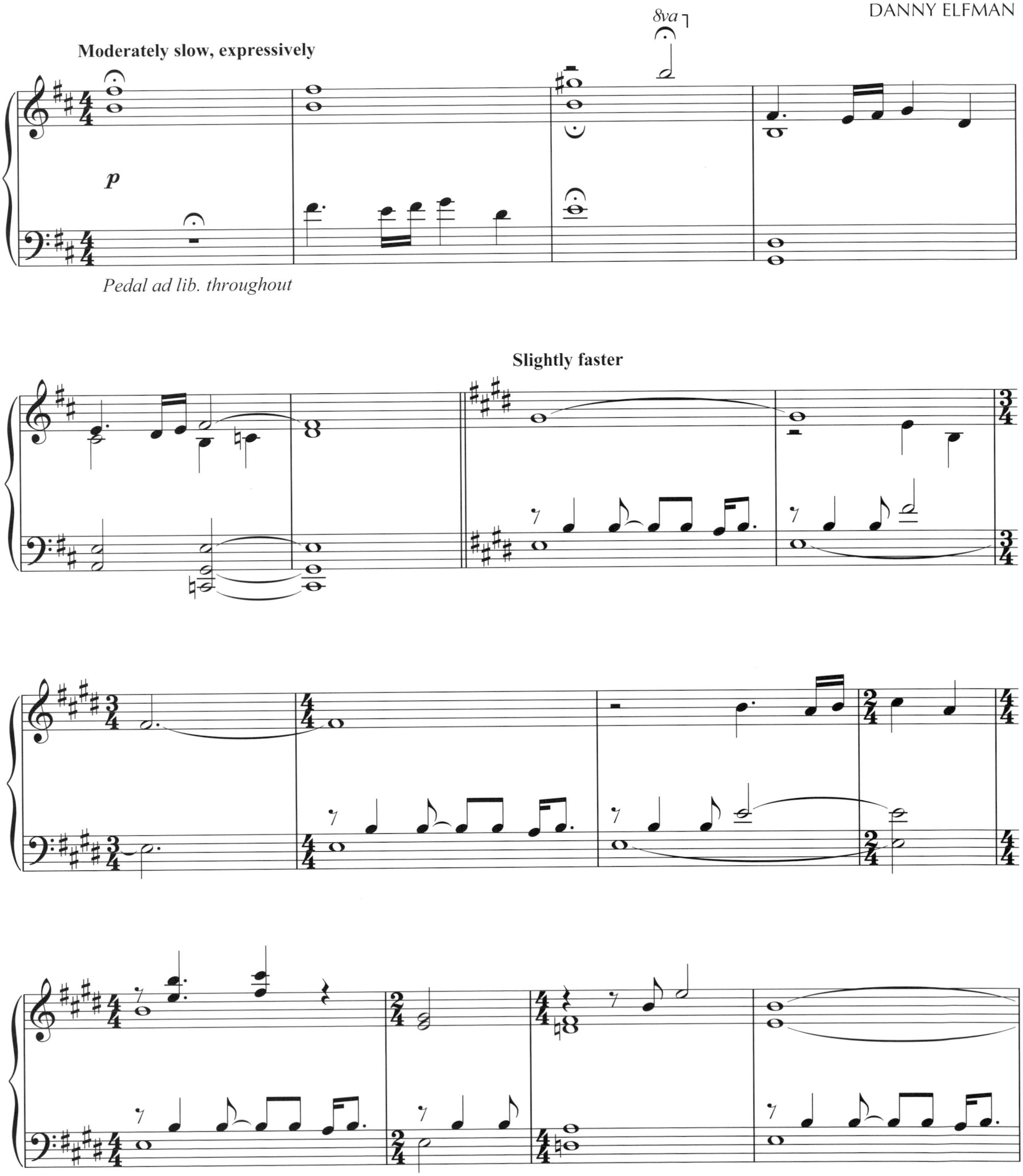

Moderately slow, expressively

Pedal ad lib. throughout

Slightly faster

© 2015 MARVEL Superheroes Music
All Rights Reserved   Used by Permission

CAN YOU STOP THIS THING?

Music by
DANNY ELFMAN

© 2015 MARVEL Superheroes Music
All Rights Reserved   Used by Permission

THE MISSION

Music by
BRIAN TYLER

Moderately

© 2015 MARVEL Superheroes Music
All Rights Reserved Used by Permission

WISH YOU WERE HERE

Music by
BRIAN TYLER

Slowly, expressively

Pedal ad lib. throughout

Moderately, steadily

© 2015 MARVEL Superheroes Music
All Rights Reserved   Used by Permission

AVENGERS UNITE

Music by
DANNY ELFMAN

© 2015 MARVEL Superheroes Music
All Rights Reserved   Used by Permission

NOTHING LASTS FOREVER

Music by
DANNY ELFMAN

© 2015 MARVEL Superheroes Music
All Rights Reserved   Used by Permission

THE LAST ONE

Music by
BRIAN TYLER

Moderately slow, expressively

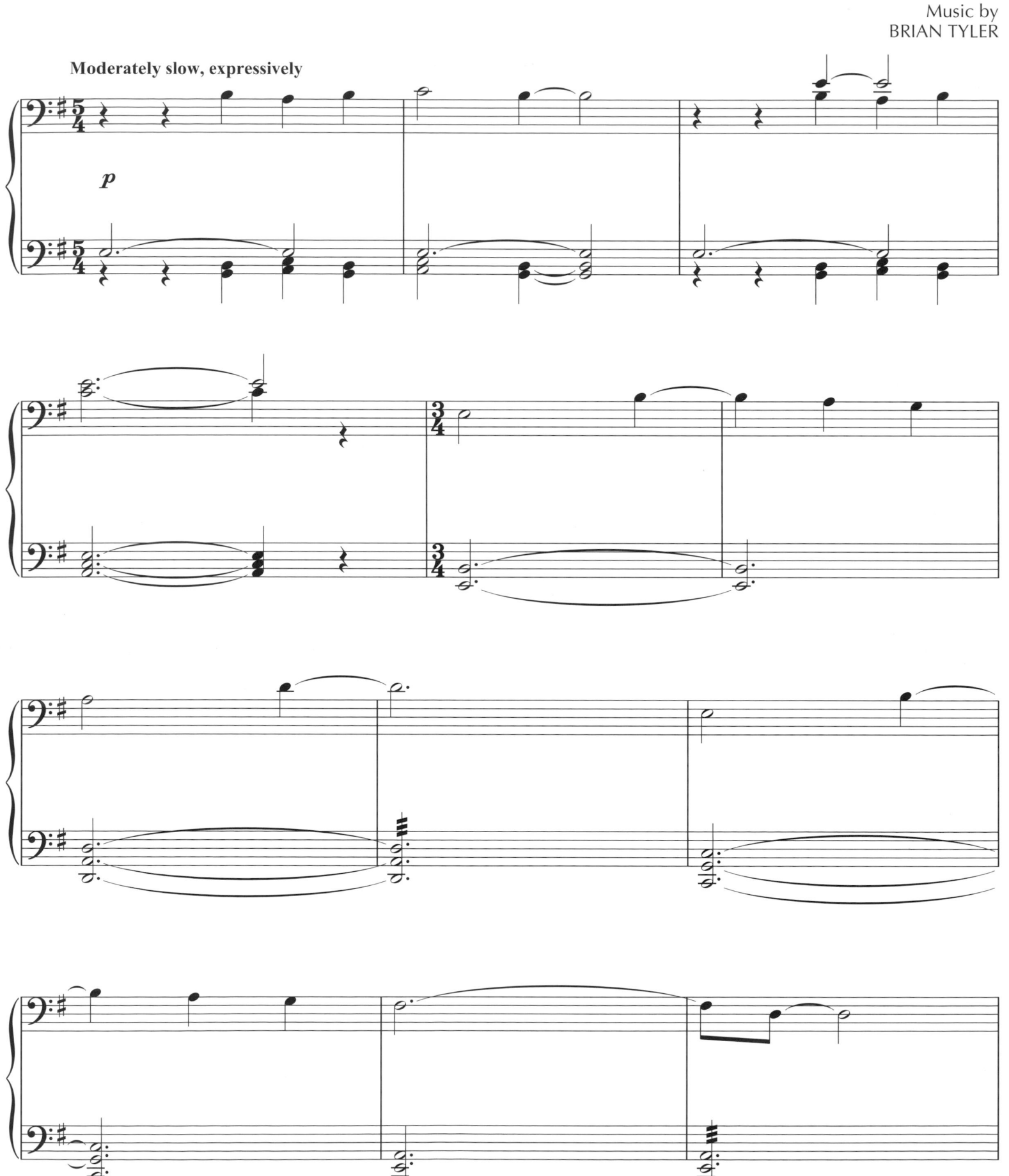

© 2015 MARVEL Superheroes Music
All Rights Reserved   Used by Permission

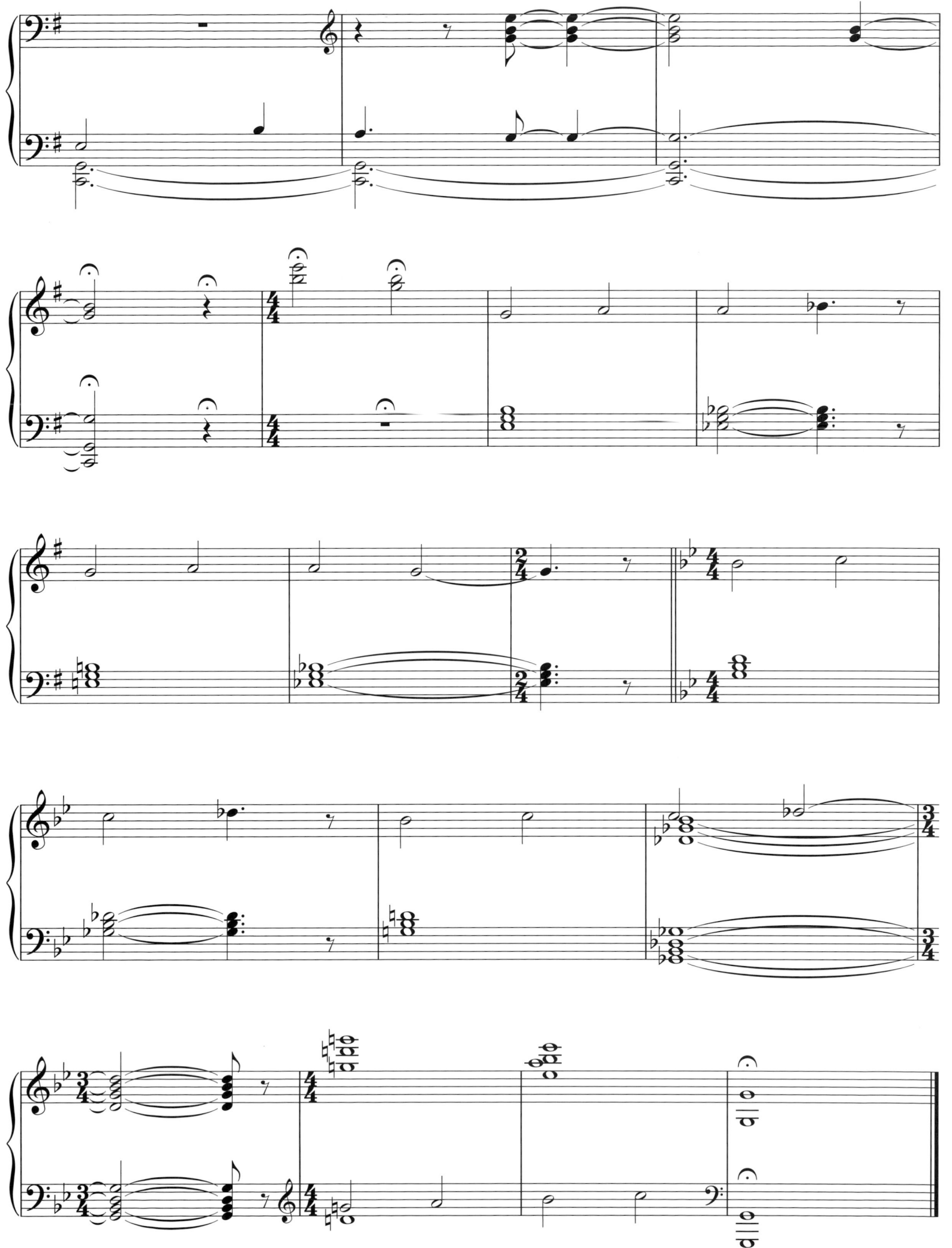

NEW AVENGERS– AVENGERS: AGE OF ULTRON

Music by
DANNY ELFMAN

Slowly, expressively

Moderately, in 2, steadily

© 2015 MARVEL Superheroes Music
All Rights Reserved   Used by Permission

Moderately fast